MAYER SMITH

Spellbound by the Nightfall

Copyright © 2025 by Mayer Smith

All rights reserved. No part of this publication may be reproduced, stored or transmitted in any form or by any means, electronic, mechanical, photocopying, recording, scanning, or otherwise without written permission from the publisher. It is illegal to copy this book, post it to a website, or distribute it by any other means without permission.

This novel is entirely a work of fiction. The names, characters and incidents portrayed in it are the work of the author's imagination. Any resemblance to actual persons, living or dead, events or localities is entirely coincidental.

Mayer Smith asserts the moral right to be identified as the author of this work.

Mayer Smith has no responsibility for the persistence or accuracy of URLs for external or third-party Internet Websites referred to in this publication and does not guarantee that any content on such Websites is, or will remain, accurate or appropriate.

Designations used by companies to distinguish their products are often claimed as trademarks. All brand names and product names used in this book and on its cover are trade names, service marks, trademarks and registered trademarks of their respective owners. The publishers and the book are not associated with any product or vendor mentioned in this book. None of the companies referenced within the book have endorsed the book.

First edition

This book was professionally typeset on Reedsy. Find out more at reedsy.com

Contents

1	The Curse of Nightfall	1
2	Secrets in the Shadows	7
3	Beneath the Surface	14
4	The Moonlit Revelation	21
5	The Shadow's Embrace	28
6	A Night of Secrets	34
7	The Betrayal	41
8	Moonlit Shadows	48
9	The Final Confrontation	55
10	The Ultimate Choice	61
11	The Dawn of Freedom	68
12	Beyond the Nightfall	74

One

The Curse of Nightfall

⁓⃝⃝⃝⃝⁓

The town of Harrow's Edge sat at the edge of the world, or at least, that's how it felt to Lila as she stood at the threshold of her new life. The wind whispered through the trees, its eerie breath curling around her ankles as if coaxing her into the shadowed depths of the forest. She had never been one for superstition, but something about this place unsettled her in ways she couldn't quite name. The way the sky hung so low at twilight, the air thick with the weight of secrets, made the town feel suspended in time.

Harrow's Edge was a place where daylight never seemed to last. The sun was an unreliable visitor, always dipping below the horizon too quickly, leaving a lingering twilight in its wake. It was as though the night fell harder here, creeping up on every house, every corner, like a living thing. And then there were the trees—the towering, twisted oaks and pines that surrounded the town like ancient sentinels. They blocked out the sky and held their secrets close.

Lila had come to Harrow's Edge for a fresh start. Or so she told herself. After the chaos of the city, the noise, the people, the suffocating demands of her life there, she needed solitude. Peace. A place where she could escape the whispering shadows of her past. The town was small—too small for anyone to notice her. It was the perfect place to disappear, to become someone else, or to simply be alone.

Yet, the moment she arrived, she felt the unmistakable pulse of something else beneath the surface. It was in the way the locals glanced at her—half wary, half curious, as if they already knew something about her that she hadn't yet learned. And it was in the way the town itself seemed to hold its breath as she stepped onto its soil.

Lila's footsteps echoed down the cobbled street, the sound unnervingly loud in the quiet town. The buildings here were older than anything she'd ever seen—a patchwork of crooked homes and crumbling stone walls, their wooden shutters sagging like tired eyelids. She passed an old shop with a faded sign hanging from a rusted chain: Moonlit Curiosities. The shop window was dark, but there was a faint flicker of light behind the glass.

Her heart skipped a beat. The name alone felt wrong, too familiar, as though it had been etched into her soul long before she'd ever heard of Harrow's Edge.

The Curse of Nightfall

A shadow darted across the street ahead, breaking her trance.

Lila paused, narrowing her eyes. Her breath caught as a figure emerged from the alley—a man, tall and unnervingly graceful. His silhouette was sharp against the backdrop of the dimming sky, his features obscured by the gathering dusk. He moved toward her, slow, deliberate, as if he knew she was watching.

And then, in the stillness of the evening, his gaze found hers.

Dorian.

His eyes were the color of midnight, deep and unblinking, and for a moment, Lila couldn't breathe. He had an almost otherworldly presence, his features drawn with an intensity that made the air feel heavy, like a storm waiting to break. He wore an old coat, the collar turned up against the chill, and though his appearance was striking, it wasn't his looks that held her captive—it was the sense of something ancient, something dangerous, lingering beneath the surface.

He stopped a mere foot away, his dark gaze never leaving hers.

"I've seen you," he said, his voice low, rough, like the sound of leaves stirring in the wind.

Lila blinked, her pulse quickening. "I don't think we've met."

He smirked, a wisp of something unreadable crossing his face. "Not in this life."

Her heart stuttered. She took a step back, unsure of whether to retreat or to stand her ground. "I—"

"You're not from here," he interrupted, his gaze sweeping over her with an intensity that made her skin tingle. "You don't belong."

The words hit her like a cold gust of wind. Something about his tone—almost predatory, yet curiously familiar—sent a ripple of unease through her. She could feel the pull of something deep inside, a recognition that didn't make sense. She had no idea who this man was, but there was something in the way he looked at her that made her blood hum with awareness.

"I'm just passing through," she said, her voice sounding far steadier than she felt. "I'm looking for a place to stay."

He took a step closer, and despite every instinct telling her to walk away, Lila didn't move. She couldn't. His presence was magnetic, pulling her in like the moon pulls the tide.

"You'll find it," he said, his lips curving into a smile that was both dangerous and comforting. "But don't say I didn't warn you."

Before she could respond, he was gone, vanishing into the shadows as effortlessly as if he had never been there at all.

Lila stood frozen for a moment, trying to collect herself, trying to breathe, but it felt as if the air had thickened around her. Her heart hammered in her chest, the weight of his words pressing down on her. *You don't belong.*

It was the second time she'd heard that phrase in less than a day, and the first had been from the strange old woman who had greeted her as she entered the town—a woman with eyes like black pools who had pulled her aside as she walked past the church. *Beware the nightfall,* the woman had whispered, her voice a rasping warning. *The curse of Harrow's Edge is not just for the dead. It follows those who dare to remain.*

Lila shook her head, brushing the thought away. She had to be imagining things. There was no curse. There was no danger. Dorian was just another strange man in a strange town.

But the unease gnawed at her as she made her way to the small bed-and-breakfast she'd reserved. She passed more houses, their windows dark and silent, as if the entire town had already settled into its own shadowed existence.

As she reached the entrance, she felt a shiver creep up her spine. The night had fully claimed the sky, the first stars twinkling faintly above. Lila could almost feel them watching her, as though the very heavens knew something she didn't.

The door creaked as she entered the dimly lit foyer. The smell of old wood and faint incense lingered in the air.

The innkeeper, an elderly woman with a warm smile and kind eyes, greeted her and showed her to her room. But as Lila stepped across the threshold, something tugged at the back of her mind, something deep and primal.

There was no escaping the feeling that she was being drawn into something far darker than she could understand.

That night, as the wind howled outside and the shadows danced against her window, Lila lay in bed wide awake, staring at the ceiling. She couldn't shake the feeling that she was being watched. That, somewhere in the deep, she was tethered to the town, to the curse, to Dorian.

The night was long. And she knew, somehow, that the curse of Harrow's Edge was just beginning to unfold.

Two

Secrets in the Shadows

Lila's first morning in Harrow's Edge arrived with a peculiar quietness, as if the sun itself was hesitant to break through the gray clouds lingering over the town. The air was damp with the scent of moss and earth, a lingering promise of rain that never fully materialized. From the small window of her room, she could see the dense forest that surrounded the town, its towering trees like sentinels watching her every move. Their branches reached out like skeletal fingers, brushing the sky in a tangled dance that seemed to defy the wind.

She lingered by the window for a moment, her fingers resting on the cool glass, her thoughts tangled with the encounter from the night before. Dorian's eyes. The way he had looked at her—like he knew something about her that she couldn't understand. The words he had spoken echoed in her mind, a warning that settled deep in her chest, making her heart race for reasons she couldn't explain.

"You don't belong."

She couldn't shake the feeling that those words held more weight than a simple insult. There was something ancient in the way he said it, as though he had seen her, truly seen her, in a way no one ever had. It was unsettling, but also… intoxicating.

The innkeeper, a plump woman named Mrs. Eddington, had made her a breakfast of warm bread, jam, and freshly brewed tea. It was simple but comforting. Still, Lila found it hard to focus on the food. Her mind kept returning to Dorian—his presence lingering in the air like the scent of a storm.

As she finished her meal, she glanced at the clock on the wall. It was nearly noon, and she had decided that today would be the day she would explore Harrow's Edge further. She needed to make sense of the strange feelings swirling inside her. Something in this town—something dark—called to her, and she couldn't ignore it.

Lila stepped outside into the cold, the air sharp against her skin as the wind picked up, biting at her exposed arms. The town was still, too still. The streets, though lined with quaint little houses and crooked storefronts, seemed to hold their breath. The cobblestones beneath her feet felt uneven, like the town itself was built atop something ancient, something that refused to be forgotten.

She made her way toward the small town square, the silence almost oppressive around her. Her footsteps echoed in the narrow streets, the sound far too loud against the quiet, like a foreign rhythm disrupting a long-held pattern. As she passed the Moonlit Curiosities shop again, she couldn't resist the pull. The flickering light behind the glass window still intrigued her, like a whisper she couldn't ignore.

She reached for the door handle, hesitating for just a moment before pushing it open. The bell above the door tinkled softly, announcing her presence.

The shop was dim, the air thick with the scent of incense and old wood. Shelves lined the walls, filled with an assortment of oddities—faded books with cracked spines, glass bottles filled with strange liquids, and trinkets that seemed to shimmer with a light of their own. But it wasn't the objects that drew her attention. It was the figure behind the counter.

A man stood there, tall and narrow-shouldered, with dark hair that fell in loose waves around his face. His eyes were the same midnight black as Dorian's, intense and unblinking, though this man's gaze lacked the heat that had sparked between her and Dorian. Instead, there was something colder, more calculating, as though he was measuring her every move.

"Can I help you, miss?" His voice was soft, but there was an edge to it, a subtle undertone that sent a shiver down her spine.

Lila cleared her throat, forcing herself to speak. "I was just—looking around."

The man's lips twitched into a slight smile, though there was no warmth in it. "Most people come in here for the curiosities. Few come to find answers."

Lila hesitated, her curiosity piqued. "Answers to what?"

"Answers to why this town keeps its secrets," he said, his voice low. "Answers to why some things are better left unsaid."

Lila's heart skipped a beat. His words felt like a warning, like something she wasn't supposed to know. But she couldn't resist. The need to understand this place, to uncover its mysteries, was consuming her.

"I don't understand," she said, taking a step closer to the counter, her fingers brushing against a glass vial filled with what looked like powdered silver.

The man's gaze flickered down to her hand, and then back to her eyes. His smile deepened, but it was more of a knowing smirk than an expression of friendliness. "You will," he said softly. "You'll understand everything, in time. But be careful, miss. The truth here... it's not something you can walk away from."

Lila swallowed hard, an uneasy feeling settling in her gut. She wasn't sure why, but something about this man made her want to leave. And yet, something deeper—some force she couldn't explain—held her in place. She opened her mouth to speak, but before she could find the right words, the door to the shop opened behind her with a sudden rush of wind.

She turned to find Dorian standing in the doorway.

His presence was immediate, overwhelming, as if the air itself shifted with his arrival. He wore the same dark coat, his collar turned up against the wind. His gaze locked onto hers, intense and searching. His lips parted as if he were about to speak, but then he seemed to hesitate, his expression flickering with a mix of caution and something else—a raw emotion she couldn't quite place.

The man behind the counter's expression hardened at the sight of Dorian, his eyes narrowing ever so slightly. "Ah, the prodigal son returns."

Dorian didn't respond at first, his gaze never leaving Lila. His voice, when it came, was low and tinged with something dangerous. "I see you've found your way into trouble, Lila."

Lila's breath hitched. "What are you talking about?"

Dorian stepped into the shop, his presence filling the small space like a shadow. The door slammed shut behind him, cutting off the outside world. "Stay away from him," Dorian said, his tone colder than she had ever heard it.

Lila took a step back, her pulse quickening as the tension between the two men grew palpable. She didn't understand what was happening, but she could feel it—there was something darker beneath the surface of this town, and it had a grip on Dorian. It was as if the very air was charged with something that could snap at any moment.

The man behind the counter didn't flinch at Dorian's words. "You always were a man of extremes, Dorian. But you can't stop her from learning the truth. No one can."

Dorian's eyes flashed with something dark, something ancient. "I'll make sure she does," he said, his voice cold as ice. He turned to Lila, his gaze softening ever so slightly. "Leave, Lila. You don't belong here."

But something in his voice—the desperation, the fear—tugged at her. She couldn't ignore it.

"I'm not leaving," she said, her voice trembling with an emotion she couldn't define. She wasn't sure if it was defiance or fear, but she couldn't walk away now. Not from Dorian, not from the mystery that was swallowing her whole.

For a long moment, there was only silence. Then Dorian's face twisted into something unreadable. He took a step closer, his eyes flickering with what looked like regret.

"Then you're already in too deep," he whispered, as if the words themselves were a promise of something terrible.

Lila didn't know what to say. She didn't know what to think. All she knew was that the shadows were closing in, and Dorian was at the center of it all. And she was falling deeper, no matter how hard she tried to resist.

The door opened again, this time with no wind to push it. And when Lila turned back, the man behind the counter was gone.

She looked at Dorian, her heart pounding in her chest. "What is this place?"

Dorian didn't answer. Instead, he turned toward the door and walked out, leaving Lila to follow, knowing there was no turning back now.

Three

Beneath the Surface

The rain came in sheets the following afternoon, drumming relentlessly against the windows of Lila's room. It was the kind of storm that enveloped the town in an eerie hush, the thunder distant but steady, as though the sky itself were holding its breath. She stood at the window, her fingers pressed to the cold glass, staring out at the town as it disappeared behind the gray mist. The trees in the forest, usually dark but still distinguishable, were now reduced to shadowy silhouettes, their jagged branches swaying in the wind like the bones of forgotten creatures.

The oppressive stillness of the town felt heavier now, as if the rain had muffled everything—every voice, every secret. But even as she tried to shake the sensation of unease creeping beneath her skin, she couldn't deny that the town had its hold on her. It was more than the weather, more than the strange figures she had met. There was something in the air itself, something ancient that refused to let go.

And then there was Dorian.

She couldn't stop thinking about him. His words, his touch, the way his presence consumed her without explanation. From the first moment she'd met him, she had felt as though she had stumbled into something far greater than herself. A force she couldn't comprehend, yet was drawn to with a ferocity she couldn't control. The way he had spoken to her, the way his dark eyes had held hers, made it impossible to look away, as if he were a flame and she, the moth, too weak to resist.

The door to her room creaked open, and Lila turned, half expecting Mrs. Eddington to bring her more tea or perhaps a few more unsolicited warnings about the strange happenings in town. But it was Dorian who stepped into the room, his silhouette framed by the doorway, his figure impossibly still, as if the storm itself bent around him.

Lila's breath caught in her throat. The moment their eyes met, something inside her stirred—an undeniable connection that left her dizzy.

"You shouldn't be here," he said, his voice barely above a whisper, but it carried an authority that made her pulse quicken.

Lila opened her mouth to speak, but no words came. She had so many questions, but they felt small, insignificant in the presence of Dorian. The way he looked at her—the intensity in his eyes—

seemed to pull the very air from her lungs. She swallowed hard, her hands trembling slightly as they gripped the edge of the windowsill.

"I know," she said finally, her voice hoarse, betraying the rapid beating of her heart. "But I can't leave."

For a moment, neither of them moved, as if the world itself had stopped spinning. The storm outside continued to rage, but it seemed distant now, the steady thrum of the rain melding with the quiet tension between them. Dorian's eyes darkened, and Lila saw something flash behind them—something she couldn't quite decipher.

"You don't understand," he said softly, his words heavy with meaning. "This place, this curse… it's not something you can walk away from. Not without cost."

Lila felt her chest tighten. The curse. She had heard whispers about it in the town—fragments of conversation, odd looks exchanged, a sense of impending doom that seemed to hang in the air like an invisible storm cloud. But no one had ever been direct about it. No one had told her what it truly meant.

"I don't care about the curse," she said, her voice more forceful than she intended. "I want to know why you're so afraid of it. Why you're afraid of me."

The words hung in the air, thick with unspoken truths, and for a moment, Dorian didn't respond. His gaze flickered down to the floor, his jaw tightening. The silence between them stretched long and suffocating, like a bridge that neither of them could cross.

"Lila..." His voice was a low rasp, and when he finally looked up at her, his eyes were full of something she couldn't name—something that frightened her. "There are things in this world that should remain hidden. There are things I can't let you understand. Not yet."

Lila stepped toward him, defiance lighting her chest like a flame. "I'm not leaving until I know the truth."

Dorian's expression softened, but only for a moment, before it was replaced by something darker, more dangerous. He took a step closer to her, and Lila's breath hitched in her throat as the air between them grew thick with tension. His gaze never wavered, and for the first time since meeting him, Lila felt truly vulnerable—exposed to something she wasn't sure she could handle.

"You think you want to know everything," he murmured, his voice low, like a caress, "but there are truths that will destroy you. Truths that will break you."

Lila swallowed hard, her heartbeat pulsing in her throat. "I can handle it."

Dorian's lips curved into a small, bitter smile. "No one can handle the truth of Harrow's Edge."

She stared at him, refusing to back down. There was something between them, an invisible thread that bound them together, pulling her in even as she wanted to pull away. Her mind screamed at her to run, to leave before things got worse, but her heart—her foolish, reckless heart—remained anchored to him.

"Tell me," she whispered, her voice trembling with urgency, "What happens if I stay?"

For the briefest of moments, Dorian's eyes flickered with uncertainty. The hardness in his features softened, and Lila saw something raw and exposed, something that mirrored the fear she felt within herself. But then, as if he could no longer stand the vulnerability, he closed himself off again. His expression hardened, and he stepped back, putting distance between them.

"You already know," he said quietly, his voice full of resignation. "You've felt it. The pull. The way this town doesn't let you leave, even when you try. It gets inside you, Lila. It gets inside your blood."

She shook her head, confusion and fear swirling inside her. "What are you saying?"

Dorian didn't answer. Instead, he walked to the window, his back to her. He stared out into the storm, his posture rigid, as if trying to resist some invisible force. The tension in the room was suffocating, and Lila could feel her mind racing to catch up with her heart. Every instinct screamed at her to leave, to run from him, from this place, but she didn't move. She couldn't.

"You're already bound to it," he said, his voice strained, barely audible above the sound of the rain. "The curse isn't just about the town. It's about what it calls. What it awakens in you. You don't even realize it yet, but you've already been marked. By the town. By me."

Lila's heart stuttered in her chest. She could feel the blood draining from her face as the realization slowly began to sink in. She wasn't just some outsider passing through. She had already become part of Harrow's Edge—part of its mystery, its danger. And Dorian, despite his warnings, was a part of that too.

Her voice was barely a whisper when she spoke. "What happens if I can't escape it?"

Dorian turned to face her, his expression unreadable. "Then you stay here forever, like the rest of us. Trapped in the shadows."

The words settled over her like a cold weight, and for a moment, she couldn't breathe. The pull between them—the undeniable, suffocating tension—grew stronger, and Lila felt herself stepping closer to him before she could stop herself.

"Is that what you want?" she whispered, her breath catching in her throat.

Dorian's eyes softened, just for a moment. "No," he said quietly. "But it's already too late for us."

And just like that, the storm outside seemed to reach its peak, the thunder crashing in a deafening roar, as if the heavens themselves had witnessed this moment and had chosen to unleash their fury.

Lila couldn't help but step forward, her hand reaching out as if to bridge the gap between them. But before she could touch him, before she could close the distance between them, the door to the room slammed open, and the harsh light of the storm outside flooded in.

And Dorian, with one final look—full of regret and something else she couldn't understand—turned and walked out, leaving her standing alone, her heart racing, in the storm's aftermath.

Four

The Moonlit Revelation

The town of Harrow's Edge had a rhythm all its own—one that seemed to pulse beneath the surface of everyday life, hidden in the shadows where few dared to venture. The rain had stopped, leaving the air thick with the smell of damp earth and the faint, almost sweet scent of decay. The trees seemed to whisper in the wind, their leaves shimmering in the low light of the setting sun. It was as if the whole town were alive with secrets, each corner hiding something just out of reach.

Lila stood at the edge of the forest, where the darkened treeline met the road that led into town. Her feet were still wet from the earlier rain, her boots soaked through, but she didn't care. She needed to be out here. She needed to understand what had drawn her to Harrow's Edge in the first place. And more importantly, she needed to understand Dorian.

She hadn't seen him since the night before—since that strange, painful conversation that had left her reeling with more questions than answers. After he had walked out of her room, she had spent the night awake, her mind swirling with thoughts of him, of the curse he had warned her about, of the pull between them that she could no longer ignore. She had never believed in things like fate or destiny, but the way she felt about him—about Harrow's Edge—was unlike anything she had ever known.

Her hand gripped the cold iron gate that separated the town from the woods, the metal slick with moisture from the storm. The gate creaked in protest as she pushed it open, the sound far too loud in the stillness. She stepped through, the underbrush crunching beneath her feet as she walked further into the trees. The shadows grew deeper here, the forest thick and oppressive, as though the night were already waiting to swallow her whole.

Her pulse quickened as she walked deeper into the forest, her senses heightened, her every movement tingling with the awareness that something was wrong. There was an energy in the air, a tension she couldn't explain, and it only seemed to grow stronger with every step she took. The trees closed in around her, their gnarled branches twisting like fingers reaching out to trap her, and the sky above was now a blanket of bruised purple and deep blue.

It was then that she heard it—the soft rustle of movement from behind her. She spun around, her breath catching in her throat, but the forest was empty, still, save for the wind that whipped through the trees.

The Moonlit Revelation

It was just the forest, she told herself. Just her imagination.

But she couldn't shake the feeling that she was being watched.

Taking a deep breath, Lila forced herself to continue walking, her eyes darting nervously between the trees. She had come this far, and there was no turning back now. She had to know the truth. She had to understand what Dorian had meant when he said she was "marked"—and why she felt so drawn to him, as if she were part of something bigger than herself.

As she made her way deeper into the woods, she finally found it—a small clearing bathed in the pale, silvery light of the moon. The air was thick with mist, curling like tendrils around the trunks of the trees, and in the center of the clearing stood an old stone monument, half-covered in ivy. The stones were weathered, worn down by time, and yet they held an ancient power, an energy that hummed in the air. The symbol etched into the stone was familiar—too familiar—and it made her blood run cold.

It was the same symbol she had seen in her dreams.

Lila's breath caught in her throat. She had seen it before—on the edges of her dreams, on the pages of the old book she had found in the town library. It was the symbol of the curse. The same symbol Dorian had warned her about. The same symbol that had marked her, whether she liked it or not.

She stepped closer to the monument, her fingers trembling as they brushed over the stone. The air around her seemed to crackle with energy, the hairs on the back of her neck standing on end as if something—or someone—was watching her. She closed her eyes for a moment, trying to steady her breathing, and when she opened them again, there was a figure standing in the shadows.

It was Dorian.

His eyes gleamed in the moonlight, his dark hair falling in soft waves around his face, his expression unreadable. He was watching her, his gaze intense, like he was searching for something within her—something he had hoped would stay hidden.

"You shouldn't be here," he said, his voice low, but it was laced with a tension that sent a chill down her spine. His gaze flickered to the monument, and she could see the pain in his eyes. "This place… this curse… it's not something you can run from."

Lila took a step toward him, her heart pounding in her chest. "I have to understand," she whispered, her voice barely audible. "What is this? What does it mean? Why am I here?"

Dorian's expression darkened, and for a moment, he seemed to hesitate, as if weighing something heavy in his mind. The air between them felt thick, charged with something unspoken, something that neither of them could escape. His eyes flickered down to the monument, and then back to her, his voice soft but firm.

The Moonlit Revelation

"The curse is tied to the bloodline," he said, his words slow and measured, as if he was forcing them out. "Your bloodline. And mine."

Lila's heart skipped a beat. "What do you mean?"

Dorian took a deep breath, his gaze shifting to the ground before locking onto hers once more. "The curse doesn't just affect the town. It's not just a story or a myth. It's real, Lila. It's been passed down for generations, from one bloodline to the next. And now, it's come for you."

She shook her head, her mind reeling with the implications of his words. "I don't understand. Why me? Why now?"

Dorian's gaze softened for a fleeting moment, and then, as if he could no longer bear the weight of what he was about to say, he stepped closer to her. The night seemed to close in around them, the moonlight casting long shadows over the forest floor.

"It's because you're marked," he whispered, his voice hoarse with regret. "You've always been marked. And so have I."

Lila's breath caught in her throat, her pulse thundering in her ears. "What does that mean? What does it mean for us?"

Dorian's hand reached out, his fingers brushing against her cheek in a touch so gentle it almost felt like a caress. But there was nothing soft about the look in his eyes. There was pain there. And fear.

"It means that we're bound to this curse," he said softly. "Bound to each other. Whether we like it or not."

Lila felt a shiver run down her spine. Her mind was racing, trying to process the magnitude of what Dorian was saying. She had come to Harrow's Edge seeking answers, seeking some sort of escape, but all she had found was a deeper, more dangerous mystery. She had thought she could walk away from this place, from Dorian. But now, standing in the heart of the forest with the monument looming behind her, she realized she had been wrong.

There was no escape. Not anymore.

The world around them seemed to shift, the air thick with a sense of inevitability, as if the earth itself had tilted beneath their feet. The storm clouds parted just enough to let the moon's light flood the clearing, casting an otherworldly glow over the scene. The monument behind them seemed to pulse with life, as if it, too, were watching them, waiting.

Dorian stepped closer to her, his breath mingling with hers in the cool night air. "We can't fight this," he murmured, his voice barely a whisper. "We can't escape what's been set in motion. But we can choose how we face it."

Lila's heart fluttered in her chest as the weight of his words sank in. She didn't know what to say. She didn't know what to do. But one thing was certain: whatever happened next, she was in this—this curse, this town, and this dangerous, consuming connection with Dorian. There was no turning back.

The Moonlit Revelation

The night deepened around them, the forest holding its breath, and for the first time since arriving in Harrow's Edge, Lila didn't feel like an outsider. She felt like she was exactly where she was supposed to be.

Bound.

Five

The Shadow's Embrace

The night had a breath to it—one that was cold and suffocating. It wrapped itself around Lila like a thick, invisible cloak, the kind that pressed against her chest and made it hard to breathe. The streets of Harrow's Edge were empty, save for the faint whispers of the wind, which seemed to carry with it something ancient, something dark. The town had a pulse, but it was a beat too slow, too heavy, as though it were waiting for something to happen.

Lila moved quickly, her footsteps clicking against the cobblestones as she crossed the square. The sky above was a sliver of dark blue, tinged with the last remnants of sunset. A pale crescent moon hung low, its sickly light casting long shadows that stretched out in impossible directions, as though the night itself was alive and pulling at her with invisible strings.

The Shadow's Embrace

She had tried to avoid it, tried to ignore the growing sense of dread gnawing at the edges of her mind, but tonight was different. After everything she had learned from Dorian—after the words he had spoken about their connection, about the curse that bound them—she could no longer pretend that nothing was happening. She was part of this town, part of its secrets, its history, its fate. And Dorian... he was part of her fate, whether she liked it or not.

As she walked, her eyes darted nervously from shadow to shadow, the feeling of being watched pressing in from every side. The last few days had been a blur—dreams, visions, things she couldn't quite explain—until finally, in a moment of clarity, she had realized she needed to confront it all. To confront him. To find out just what he was hiding.

Lila's pace quickened as she neared the edge of the town, where the trees of the forest began to loom, dark and menacing. She had spent hours searching for answers, reading old books and asking questions, but the more she uncovered, the more questions she had. The curse, the bloodlines, the town's strange history—it was all connected, but the connection was like a thread pulled too tight, threatening to snap at any moment.

When she reached the edge of the forest, she paused. The trees stood like towering sentinels, their limbs twisting in the wind as though reaching for her. The shadows beneath the canopy seemed to stretch out in every direction, an impenetrable darkness that made her hesitate.

And then, like a ghost from her dreams, Dorian appeared.

His figure materialized from the trees, his dark coat blending with the night as if he had been part of it all along. His eyes gleamed in the moonlight, watching her, waiting. He didn't speak at first, but the tension between them was palpable, a silent current that thrummed through the air.

Lila's heart skipped a beat, but she didn't flinch. She couldn't. Not now.

"You're here," he said, his voice low, filled with a mixture of warning and something else—something that made her pulse quicken.

"I had to be," Lila replied, her voice steady despite the storm of emotions swirling inside her. "I need to understand. Everything. About the curse, about you, about why I'm here."

Dorian's gaze flickered to the darkened trees behind her before meeting her eyes once more. There was a rawness to his expression, something unspoken, like a truth he wasn't sure he could reveal. "You don't know what you're asking for," he said softly, his words carrying the weight of experience, of pain. "This town—it changes people. The curse...it changes everything."

"I've already changed," Lila whispered, taking a step closer, the distance between them growing shorter with every beat of her heart. "I don't know why, but something inside me—inside my blood—tells me that this place is where I belong. And you..." She hesitated, searching his eyes for answers. "You feel it too, don't you?"

Dorian's lips parted, a breath escaping his chest as if her words had taken the wind out of him. For a moment, he said nothing, simply looking at her, his eyes searching hers as though trying to gauge whether she was ready for the truth. His gaze softened, just for a fraction of a second, but in that instant, Lila saw something in him—something that mirrored the turmoil she felt inside herself. He had always been guarded, always held back, but now, in the darkness, it was as if all the walls between them were slowly beginning to crumble.

"I've never wanted this," he said, his voice thick with emotion, "but there's no escaping it. Not anymore."

The air between them grew heavy, charged with a palpable energy that made Lila's skin prickle. She didn't fully understand what he meant, but she felt the weight of his words deep in her chest, like a promise or a warning.

"You think you can just walk away from it?" she asked, her voice trembling with something fierce. "That you can just shut me out and expect it all to go away? This place, this curse, this connection between us—it's not something you can hide from. It's not something I can ignore."

He shook his head, a bitter laugh escaping his lips. "You think I don't know that? You think I haven't tried?" His voice broke, just for a moment, before he caught himself. He stepped closer to her, his presence enveloping her, the heat of his body almost too much to bear. "I've spent my whole life running from this. From the curse, from you, from the truth. But it always finds its way back. And now, so have you."

Lila's breath caught in her throat. The way he said it—now, so have you—it sounded like a sentence, like a final verdict. She felt the weight of it pressing down on her, suffocating her with the realization that there was no escaping this.

But she couldn't turn away. She wouldn't.

"What happens now?" she asked, her voice small, as if she were afraid of the answer.

Dorian reached out, his hand brushing against her cheek in a touch that was both tender and desperate. His fingers felt cold, but his gaze burned with an intensity that made Lila's heart race.

"Now," he said, his voice thick with emotion, "we face it. Together, or apart. But it's here, Lila. It's in us."

She closed her eyes, unable to process the whirlwind of emotions that surged through her. The connection between them was undeniable, as was the danger that lingered in the air. They were bound to this town, to this curse, and to each other. There was no escaping it. No running away.

Lila opened her eyes to find him closer now, his face inches from hers. She could feel the heat of his breath against her skin, and for a moment, she forgot everything—everything except the pull between them. The gravity of it was inescapable, drawing her in, urging her to close the distance, to let herself fall.

"I don't know if I'm ready for this," she whispered, her voice trembling. "But I don't think I can stop it."

Dorian's lips brushed against hers before he pulled back slightly, his breath ragged. "Neither of us can stop it," he whispered. "But we can choose how we face it."

The storm raged above them, the wind howling through the trees, but in that moment, nothing else mattered. The world could have fallen away, and it would have felt like nothing more than the space between their breaths. The kiss that followed was soft, tentative at first, as if they were both testing the waters of something forbidden, something they knew they shouldn't want but couldn't help.

And then, as the storm continued to rage around them, they gave in.

In that moment, with the wind howling and the forest pressing in around them, they were no longer two separate people, no longer bound by the curse alone. They were something else entirely—something both fragile and unbreakable.

Something bound by the shadows of the night.

Six

A Night of Secrets

The town of Harrow's Edge had taken on a strange stillness, like the calm before a storm. The usual creaks and groans of the houses settling in the night were absent, as though even the buildings themselves were holding their breath. The air was thick with the scent of damp wood and earth, but it was laced with something else—something she couldn't name, something that made the hairs on the back of her neck stand on end.

Lila stood at the window of her room, staring out into the inky night. The moon was hidden behind thick clouds, casting the world in a shadowed, impenetrable darkness. The forest stood just beyond the edge of the town, its silhouette like a dark wall, a silent sentry watching over everything. She couldn't escape the feeling that something was watching her from within it. The same sensation that had gripped her the night she had arrived in Harrow's Edge had only grown stronger with each passing hour, and now, it was almost overwhelming.

She had tried to distract herself—tried to push the dark thoughts from her mind—but it was useless. Dorian's words echoed in her ears, his warning still lingering like a bitter taste on her tongue.

"You've always been marked. And so have I."

She didn't know how, but she knew he had told her the truth. Everything about this town—the curse, the shadows, the pull between them—was real. But what did it all mean for her? What did it mean for them? She couldn't keep pretending that she wasn't tangled in something far deeper than she could possibly understand. And yet, she couldn't bring herself to leave either.

The sound of a soft knock at the door broke through her thoughts, and Lila jumped, her heart racing as she turned toward it. She hadn't been expecting anyone, not after the tense, half-formed conversation she had had with Dorian earlier that evening. But she couldn't ignore the quiet instinct that told her who it was.

Her hand shook slightly as she reached for the door, her pulse quickening with anticipation. When she opened it, Dorian stood there, his eyes dark and unreadable, his presence filling the doorway like a storm. He was drenched, the rain still falling in sheets outside, but he didn't seem to care. His hair hung in wet strands around his face, his coat heavy with moisture, but the look in his eyes was what arrested her. It was something close to desperation—something raw and aching—and it made her stomach flutter with both fear and something else she couldn't name.

"I need to speak to you," he said, his voice low, but thick with urgency.

Lila didn't move. "It's late. What's going on, Dorian?"

He stepped forward, his gaze flickering to the empty hall behind her before meeting her eyes again. "You need to come with me," he said, his voice tight. "There's no more time to waste."

Lila felt a rush of uncertainty flood her chest, but something in his eyes—something unspoken—pushed her forward. She stepped aside, and Dorian entered, his wet clothes leaving a trail of dampness on the floor. The air in the room grew heavier, the tension between them growing with each passing second. She felt it—the weight of whatever it was he was about to tell her—and the anticipation gnawed at her insides.

"Where are we going?" she asked, her voice barely a whisper.

"To the woods," he said, his gaze never leaving hers. "There's something you need to see. Something you need to know."

Before Lila could respond, he was already moving, and without another word, he took her hand, pulling her gently but firmly behind him. His touch was cold, wet, but the grip was strong—unshakable. The night outside had grown colder, and the rain seemed to have intensified, the world around them dimming as though it were already lost to shadow.

The streets of Harrow's Edge were eerily quiet as they walked, the only sound being the rhythmic pounding of their footsteps against the wet cobblestones. The town was like a ghost town now, its buildings dark and silent, the few scattered lights flickering weakly against the storm's fury. No one else was out tonight, no one else dared to step into the night when the winds howled like they did.

But it wasn't the storm or the town that occupied Lila's mind. It was Dorian. His grip on her hand never faltered, and though his expression remained inscrutable, she could feel the tension rolling off of him in waves. She could sense the battle within him—something was tearing him apart, and it had everything to do with the curse, with her.

When they reached the edge of the forest, Lila stopped, her heart pounding in her chest. The trees loomed before them, black and twisted against the sky. The air here was thicker, heavier with the scent of wet pine and damp earth, but there was something else now—something ancient, something unsettling.

"I don't understand," Lila said, her voice trembling. "Why bring me here, Dorian?"

He didn't respond immediately. Instead, he looked at the forest with a mixture of fear and longing, as if it were something he couldn't escape even though he desperately wanted to. Then, finally, his gaze met hers.

"You're not just tied to this town," he said, his voice tight with emotion. "You're tied to this place. To the curse itself."

The words sent a chill down Lila's spine, and she stepped back, pulling her hand from his. "I don't… I don't understand."

"You don't have to understand everything right now," he said urgently. "But you need to trust me. Come with me. There's something in these woods… something hidden. And it's the key to everything."

Lila hesitated. She wanted to turn away, to run, but she couldn't. There was something in his eyes, something that reached into her soul and made it impossible to say no. And so, despite the fear gnawing at her, she followed him.

They walked deeper into the forest, the trees growing thicker, their limbs twisting like arms, closing in around them as if the forest itself were alive, watching. The silence between them was deafening, the only sounds the rhythmic crunch of their footsteps on the wet ground and the distant roar of thunder.

Then, as they reached a small clearing, Dorian stopped. He let go of her hand and moved toward a large stone at the center of the clearing, his movements slow, almost reverent. The stone was old, covered in vines and moss, but there was something about it that called to Lila. Something familiar.

"This is it," Dorian said softly. "This is where it all started."

Lila moved closer, drawn to the stone like a magnet, but

something stopped her—an unnatural sensation creeping up her spine. The ground beneath her feet seemed to hum, a low vibration that made her dizzy. She reached out a hand to touch the stone, and the moment her fingers brushed the cold surface, a surge of energy shot through her. The vision came instantly—flashes of faces, of places, of things she couldn't understand.

And in the center of it all, a figure—a woman with eyes like hers—reached out, beckoning.

Lila gasped, pulling her hand away from the stone, her breath coming in short, sharp bursts. She turned to Dorian, but the words wouldn't come. The vision had been so real, so vivid, that she couldn't shake the feeling that she had just seen something she was never supposed to.

Dorian stood behind her, his face pale, his eyes wide with fear. "You've seen it, haven't you?" he asked, his voice hoarse.

"I don't know," Lila whispered. "I... I don't understand what I saw."

"That was the truth," Dorian said, his voice thick with emotion. "The truth about the curse. About you. About us. Your bloodline—it's always been tied to this place. To the ritual. To the curse. And now..." He paused, his gaze flickering to the trees, then back to her. "Now it's your turn."

Lila's heart pounded in her chest, her mind racing to process everything. She felt as though the ground had shifted beneath her, as though the entire world was tilting and she was falling into it, deeper and deeper, until she couldn't breathe.

"Your turn?" she whispered, her voice barely audible. "What do you mean?"

Dorian didn't answer immediately. Instead, he took a step toward her, his eyes searching hers. There was something in his gaze—a darkness, a despair—that made her chest tighten.

"You've always been meant for this, Lila," he said softly. "And now, there's no turning back."

The wind howled through the trees, and the world around them seemed to darken, the shadows closing in as if to swallow them whole. Lila's heart pounded in her chest, and she felt the weight of what Dorian had said press down on her like a vice. There was no escape from this, no turning back. She had been marked. And now, it was her turn.

Seven

The Betrayal

T he town of Harrow's Edge was swallowed whole by the night, the moon hidden behind a thick veil of clouds. The streets were deserted, the cobblestones slick with moisture from the rain that had fallen earlier. The wind howled through the trees, carrying with it an unsettling chill, as though the forest itself was whispering secrets—secrets Lila wasn't ready to hear.

She had spent the day in a haze, her mind reeling from everything she had seen and heard. Dorian's words still echoed in her ears, heavy and haunting. "Now it's your turn."

The weight of the curse hung over her like a shadow, suffocating and relentless. She had never believed in fate or destiny, but now, in this town that seemed to breathe with dark power, she could feel the pull. The pull of the curse. The pull of Dorian.

But there was something else, something gnawing at her. A feeling of being trapped, of being led down a path that she couldn't escape. She wanted answers, but the deeper she went, the more questions arose. The truth seemed just out of reach, always shifting, always changing.

Lila stood by the window in her room, staring out into the darkness. The wind tugged at the curtains, making them flutter like ghostly wings. The trees swayed in the distance, their branches creaking in protest as the storm intensified. She could hear the faintest sound of footsteps from below, a rhythmic pattern that she recognized but couldn't quite place.

And then, as if summoned by the storm itself, Dorian appeared at the door, his presence like a shadow in the dimly lit room. He didn't knock; he simply stepped inside, closing the door softly behind him. The scent of the rain still clung to his coat, and his eyes—those dark, fathomless eyes—locked onto hers with an intensity that made her pulse quicken.

"You came," he said, his voice low and rough. "I thought you might run."

Lila didn't respond immediately. Her chest tightened with the emotions she couldn't quite name. The air between them was thick with unspoken words, the tension hanging heavy as if the very atmosphere had grown charged with the promise of something inevitable. Something dangerous.

"I didn't run," she said finally, her voice steady but filled with an emotion she couldn't hide. "I'm here because I need to

The Betrayal

understand. You've shown me bits and pieces of this curse, Dorian. But you're holding back. What aren't you telling me?"

Dorian stepped further into the room, his gaze never leaving hers. There was something different about him tonight—something darker. The walls that had seemed so impenetrable before were beginning to crack, revealing the edges of something more sinister beneath.

"I'm not hiding anything from you," he said, his voice tinged with frustration. "But there are things that are better left unsaid. You don't know what you're asking for, Lila."

Lila's breath caught in her throat. "I need to know everything," she whispered. "I can't keep living in the dark. I can't keep pretending that this—this connection we have—doesn't mean something."

For a moment, Dorian's expression softened, his gaze flickering with something like regret. His hand twitched at his side, but he didn't reach for her. Not yet.

"I didn't want this for you," he said quietly, his voice barely audible against the howling wind outside. "I never wanted you to be part of this. The curse—it's too dangerous. It's not something you can just walk away from."

Lila felt her pulse quicken at his words. "I don't have a choice, do I?" she asked, the words slipping from her mouth before she could stop them.

Dorian's eyes darkened. "No," he said, his voice tight with something close to anger. "You don't. But there are things you don't understand yet. Things that—" He stopped, his eyes narrowing as if he were searching for the right words. "Things that will change everything."

Before Lila could ask what he meant, there was a sudden, loud knock at the door. The sound broke through the tension like a crack of thunder, and for a moment, everything seemed to freeze. Lila looked at Dorian, her heart pounding in her chest.

"Who is it?" she asked, her voice barely a whisper.

Dorian's expression darkened even further. He moved swiftly to the door, his hand on the knob, but before he could open it, he hesitated. He looked back at Lila, his eyes filled with something unreadable.

"You don't know what's coming," he said urgently. "You need to stay away from the door."

But before he could reach her, the door was thrown open, and a figure stepped into the room.

Lila gasped. The man standing in the doorway was someone she recognized, but barely—a tall, imposing figure with sharp features and dark eyes. It was Isaac, the man she had met briefly when she first arrived in Harrow's Edge. But he looked different now. His clothes were torn, his face bruised, his eyes wild with fear.

The Betrayal

"Dorian!" Isaac's voice was rough, desperate. "They've found us. It's too late."

Dorian's eyes flashed with a mix of disbelief and anger. "I told you to stay out of it, Isaac," he said, his voice tight with frustration.

Isaac stumbled into the room, his breath coming in ragged gasps. He collapsed onto the floor, his hands trembling as he reached for Dorian. "You don't understand. It's not just the curse. It's the Order—they've been watching us. They know about her."

Lila's heart skipped a beat as she took a step back. "What do you mean? What are you talking about?"

Dorian moved quickly, his face a mask of cold determination. "You shouldn't have come here, Isaac. You've put us all at risk."

Isaac looked up at him, fear clouding his features. "It's too late. They've already started the ritual. They're going to use her, Dorian. They're going to use her to complete it."

The words hit Lila like a blow to the chest. Her mind raced to make sense of them, but they felt like a jumble of confusion and fear. She turned to Dorian, her voice trembling with shock. "What's happening? What ritual? What do they want with me?"

Dorian didn't meet her eyes. He was staring at Isaac with an expression of rage that she had never seen before. "I didn't think they'd find us this soon," he muttered, his voice low and filled with bitterness. "The Order doesn't play by the same rules as the rest of us. And they've been hunting you for a long time, Lila."

Lila felt her stomach twist, her head spinning with the implications of what Isaac had said. "The Order?" she whispered. "What Order?"

Isaac's eyes darted nervously around the room, as if expecting someone to burst through the door at any moment. "They're the ones who control everything in Harrow's Edge," he explained, his voice shaking with fear. "They've been pulling the strings for centuries. And now... they've found her."

Dorian finally turned to face her, his eyes dark with regret. "I didn't want you to get involved in this," he said quietly. "But now... now you're a part of it, whether you like it or not."

Lila's chest tightened with a mixture of confusion and something darker—something she couldn't explain. "I don't understand," she whispered. "What do they want with me?"

"They want to use you to finish the ritual," Dorian said softly, his voice filled with an edge of pain. "You're the key, Lila. You always have been. And now, they'll do whatever it takes to get to you."

The room seemed to close in around her as the truth settled like a heavy stone in her chest. The air grew thick with the weight of the words, the air heavy with danger. The storm outside raged even louder now, the thunder crashing in the distance like the heartbeat of a world that was collapsing.

The Betrayal

Lila's heart pounded in her chest. "How do we stop them?" she asked, her voice barely a whisper.

Dorian looked at her, his expression unreadable. "We don't. Not unless we're willing to make the ultimate sacrifice."

Lila's breath caught in her throat. She could feel the weight of his words like a noose tightening around her neck. And as she stared at Dorian, she realized with horrifying clarity that there was no escaping this. There was no way out.

The ritual was coming. And there was nothing she could do to stop it.

Eight

Moonlit Shadows

The night felt different, as though the earth itself was holding its breath. The storm had passed, but the air still felt charged, alive with something dark, something ancient. The clouds parted slowly, revealing the full moon, its cold light washing over Harrow's Edge in a spectral glow. The trees in the forest trembled in the breeze, their branches swaying as though whispering to each other, sharing secrets that only the night could understand.

Lila stood in the doorway of the small inn, her gaze fixed on the distant trees, a swirling vortex of thoughts and emotions crashing in her chest. The truth had come crashing down on her all at once—the ritual, the Order, the bloodlines. She had always known something was wrong in Harrow's Edge, but now, she was at the center of it. The weight of that knowledge pressed down on her, suffocating and yet, strangely, undeniable.

Moonlit Shadows

She had never believed in fate or destiny, but she couldn't ignore the pull now. The curse was real. And she was a part of it.

Her fingers clenched around the cold wood of the doorframe, and she took a deep breath, trying to steady herself. The world around her had become a place of shifting shadows, and there was no way to turn back. Not now. Not after what Isaac had said, after the look in Dorian's eyes as he told her about the ritual.

She wasn't sure how long she stood there, lost in the storm inside her mind, but the soft scrape of boots against stone broke the silence. She turned, her heart jumping in her chest.

Dorian stood just inside the doorway, his wet hair clinging to his forehead, his coat heavy with the dampness of the storm. He looked as though he had stepped out of the shadows themselves, his expression unreadable, his eyes dark with something unreadable. His presence filled the room in a way that left no room for anything else.

Lila didn't know what to say. She wanted to ask him everything, to demand answers, but the look in his eyes made her pause. There was pain there. Regret. A silent admission that things had gone too far, and now, there was no turning back.

"You shouldn't be out here," he said, his voice low, rough with the strain of something unsaid. "It's dangerous."

Lila didn't flinch. "What's happening, Dorian?" she whispered. "What did Isaac mean? What is the ritual? What do they want with me?"

Dorian's gaze flickered toward the forest, as though he could feel the weight of the trees, the heavy silence pressing in from every side. His jaw clenched, and he turned to face her, his eyes dark with something she couldn't name.

"They want you, Lila," he said, his voice thick with a bitter edge. "The Order doesn't care about anything else. The ritual is the only thing that matters to them. And you're at the heart of it. You always have been."

Her breath caught in her throat as his words settled like a heavy stone in her chest. She could feel the weight of it—the truth crashing down on her like a wave, pulling her under, drowning her in the suffocating darkness.

"But why me?" she asked, her voice barely a whisper. "Why now?"

Dorian's eyes softened, the darkness in them deepening as he stepped closer to her, his presence wrapping around her like a vice. "Because you're the one who can break the curse," he said quietly. "You're the one who can end it. Or make it worse."

The air in the room thickened, the space between them shrinking until it felt as though they were the only two people left in the world. The intensity in his gaze was enough to make her heart race, but it was the weight of his words that made her stomach twist. The ritual wasn't just about her. It was about the fate of the town, of everything it had become, everything it was tied to.

And Dorian—he was tied to it too.

"You don't have to do this," she said, her voice trembling. "There has to be another way."

Dorian didn't answer immediately. He stepped closer to her, so close that she could feel the heat radiating off his body, his breath a soft whisper against her ear. The moment felt suspended in time, as though the world itself had frozen in anticipation.

"There is no other way," he murmured, his hand reaching out to touch her face, his fingers tracing the curve of her cheek. The warmth of his touch burned through her skin, searing her with the same intensity she had felt the first time they touched. "You were always meant for this. And so was I."

Her heart pounded in her chest as she looked up at him, searching his eyes for some sign, some clue that this was all a mistake—that they could still walk away from this. But the darkness in his gaze told her everything she needed to know. There was no turning back.

"I don't want this," she whispered, her voice shaking with the weight of everything that had happened. "I don't want to be a part of the curse. I don't want to be the one who ends it."

Dorian's expression softened, but it wasn't the softness she had hoped for. It was the sadness of someone who had known all along that this moment was coming—that there had never been any other path to walk but this one.

"You don't get to choose," he said, his voice thick with regret. "None of us do. But you're stronger than you know, Lila. And together, we can stop it. We can break the curse."

Lila's heart clenched in her chest as she looked at him, really looked at him, for the first time since all of this had begun. He was right. There was no choice left. No easy way out.

But the thought of breaking the curse—of ending everything that had come before her, everything that had bound her to this town, to Dorian—left a hollow ache deep in her chest.

"We'll do it together, won't we?" she whispered, her voice barely audible, her words caught somewhere between hope and despair. "We'll break the curse. Together."

Dorian's gaze softened, and for a moment, he was the man she had first met—the man she had trusted, the man who had promised her safety. But the shadows were still there, lurking just beneath the surface, and she knew, deep down, that nothing was ever going to be simple again.

"We will," he said softly, his voice full of determination. "But you have to understand, Lila. There are things you don't know. Things I haven't told you."

The air in the room seemed to grow colder, the weight of his words pressing in around her. Lila's pulse quickened as she looked at him, searching for the truth in his eyes. "What are you hiding?" she asked, her voice barely a whisper.

Dorian hesitated, and in that moment, Lila knew something was wrong. She could feel it in the tension of his shoulders, in the way his gaze shifted toward the door as though expecting someone to walk in. He was hiding something—something even darker than the curse, something that would change everything.

"I've been trying to protect you," he said quietly, his voice strained with the weight of his own secrets. "From everything. From myself."

Lila's breath caught in her throat. She took a step back, her mind reeling with the implications of his words. What was he trying to protect her from? What was he keeping from her?

Before she could respond, a noise from outside the door broke the silence. The unmistakable sound of footsteps—slow, deliberate, echoing in the stillness. Lila's heart stopped, her breath caught in her chest as she turned toward the door.

Dorian's hand shot out to stop her from moving, his grip firm and urgent. "Don't open it," he said, his voice low, filled with fear. "You don't know who's out there."

Lila's mind raced, but she didn't move. The footsteps were closer now, and the air seemed to hum with the promise of something terrible, something that was about to shatter everything they had fought for.

And as the door creaked open, Lila knew in that moment that nothing would ever be the same again.

Nine

The Final Confrontation

The door creaked open slowly, its hinges groaning as if reluctant to give way. Lila's heart pounded in her chest, each beat echoing in her ears, too loud, too fast. The cold air from the hallway poured into the room, sharp and unwelcoming. Her breath hitched as her eyes darted to Dorian, his face etched with an intensity that left no room for doubt. He knew something she didn't. Something dangerous.

The footsteps outside the door had stopped, but the silence was only momentary. Then came the sharp knock—the sound so final, so chilling, that it felt like the echo of a death knell.

Dorian's hand tightened on her wrist, pulling her a fraction closer, his grip strong but not painful. "Stay behind me," he whispered, his voice rough with urgency. "Whatever happens, don't make a sound. Do you understand?"

Lila didn't answer. Her body moved without thought, instinctively falling into place behind him, her back pressed against the cool stone wall as she held her breath, waiting for the next movement, the next sound. Her pulse surged in her throat, and every instinct screamed at her to run, to get out of the room before whatever was coming entered.

Another knock. A bit louder this time, as though the visitor was impatient. And then the door opened, just enough for a sliver of moonlight to cut through the darkened room. The figure in the doorway was tall, draped in the shadows, the outline of their face hidden beneath the brim of a wide hat. A cloak, dark as the night itself, swirled around their form, blending into the gloom.

For a heartbeat, no one moved. The only sound in the room was the breath they were all holding—Dorian, Lila, and the stranger standing in the doorway. Lila's skin prickled, an overwhelming sense of dread washing over her. She could feel the weight of the presence in the room—the oppressive energy that clung to every corner, suffocating in its finality.

"You've been hiding her well, Dorian," a low voice said, calm and smooth, but with an undercurrent of something dark, something chilling. "But it's time for her to come with us."

Lila's heart skipped. The words landed like a slap, the meaning far too clear. The Order. They had found her. And there was no escape.

Dorian's jaw tightened, his hand still gripping her wrist with a

The Final Confrontation

possessive force that told her everything she needed to know. "No," he said, his voice steady, but laced with fury. "She's not going anywhere with you."

The figure in the doorway chuckled, a dry, mirthless sound. It sent a shiver crawling up Lila's spine. The stranger took a step forward, the shadows swallowing him up as he moved. There was a smell in the air now, something metallic and bitter—a scent of old blood, of history long buried.

"You don't get to make that choice, Dorian," the stranger said, stepping closer until Lila could make out the sharp, angular lines of his face. His eyes gleamed coldly in the dim light, two pale orbs of ice that bored into hers with a hunger that chilled her to the core. "You've made your choice. And so has she."

Lila's heart lurched. She knew that voice. She knew those eyes. But it was impossible.

"Isaac?" she whispered, her voice barely audible, as if saying his name aloud might shatter the fragile illusion she had been clinging to.

Isaac's lips curled into a smile, a smile that was too wide, too cruel. "Surprised to see me, Lila? I'm afraid you've been too busy listening to Dorian to realize who you really belong to."

Dorian stepped forward, his hand still gripping Lila's, but now there was a fierceness to his movements, a wild, desperate energy that she hadn't seen before. "Stay back, Isaac," he growled, his voice low and guttural. "This is your last chance to walk away. You know what happens if you push me."

Isaac's smile faltered, replaced by something more menacing. "I don't need to walk away, Dorian," he said, his voice cutting through the air like a knife. "You've always been too weak. And now, you've become part of the problem. You're the one standing in the way of the Order's future. And Lila..." He let out a soft laugh, eyes gleaming with a dark, twisted amusement. "Well, she's the key to everything."

Lila's stomach churned. She glanced at Dorian, searching his face for any sign of the man she had come to trust, the man who had made her believe she could find a way out of all this madness. But all she saw now was a stranger, someone who had been forced into a role he couldn't escape. Someone who had betrayed his own fate, and now, the consequences were here.

The room grew colder still, the shadows in the corners stretching toward them like tendrils, pulling everything into the dark. The tension in the air was palpable, thick enough to suffocate. Lila's breath came in shallow gasps, her mind a blur of confusion and dread. She could feel the weight of the truth pressing on her, suffocating her.

"You don't get to make the decisions for me," Lila said, her voice trembling but steady. She wasn't sure where the words were coming from—whether from her heart or her fear, but they felt right. "I'm not part of your game, Isaac. And neither is Dorian."

Isaac's eyes flickered with something like irritation, but he

The Final Confrontation

didn't move. Instead, he gave a slow, mocking clap. "Oh, how cute. You think you have a choice, don't you?"

Lila's chest tightened, the suffocating weight of the situation closing in on her. "I do have a choice. And I choose not to play your game. Not anymore."

Isaac's expression shifted then, his lips curling into a smirk that seemed almost predatory. "You don't get to choose, Lila. You've already made your choice. You're a part of this, and you always will be."

Dorian moved faster than she could react, his hand gripping Isaac's throat, shoving him back against the doorframe with a force that cracked the wood. "I'm done listening to your lies," he snarled, his voice low, filled with rage. "You've been pulling the strings from the shadows for too long. And it ends tonight."

Isaac's eyes narrowed, but there was no fear in them. "You think you can stop us, Dorian? You think you're the only one who has a claim on her?"

Lila's breath caught as she looked at Dorian, her mind racing. A claim? What does that even mean? The connection between them was undeniable, but this—this feeling, this fight—was something darker, something that cut deeper than anything she had ever felt.

"I don't want your power, Isaac," Dorian said, his voice deadly quiet. "I want to end this. All of it."

Isaac smirked again, the malicious gleam in his eyes sharpening. "You can't end it, Dorian. Not without the price. And she—" He turned to Lila, his gaze narrowing, "—is the price."

Everything happened at once. Isaac shoved Dorian back with a force that sent him stumbling, and Lila cried out as the space between them grew. The door behind Isaac creaked ominously as if the very walls of the room were moving to imprison them.

Lila took a step forward, but Isaac's eyes locked onto hers, and she felt it then—something dark, something cold and heavy curling in her chest, suffocating her. The power of the curse. The power of whatever dark force had bound her to this town, to Dorian, to Isaac.

"You will come with me," Isaac said, his voice a harsh whisper, "or you will destroy him. And if you do that—if you make the wrong choice—you will be the one who brings about the end."

Lila's eyes burned, her heart a frantic drumbeat in her chest as she glanced at Dorian. She had never felt so torn in her life, but in this moment, she knew: the stakes were higher than she had ever imagined. The decision she made now would change everything.

And the clock was ticking.

Ten

The Ultimate Choice

The cold winds howled through the broken window, carrying with them the scent of wet leaves and the sharp bite of winter. Harrow's Edge was quiet, too quiet, as if it were holding its breath, waiting for something terrible to happen. The room around them was dimly lit, the flickering candle casting long, warped shadows that stretched across the walls like fingers reaching toward the two figures standing at its center.

Lila stood frozen, her heart racing, her mind a whirlwind of confusion, fear, and disbelief. Isaac's words hung in the air like a curse, each syllable more suffocating than the last. "You're a part of this. You've always been. And now, there's no turning back."

Her gaze flickered to Dorian, standing just a few feet away, his chest rising and falling with ragged breaths, his fists clenched at his sides. His eyes were full of something—pain, regret, perhaps even fear—but there was something else there too, something raw, something dangerous.

In that moment, standing between the two men, she could feel the weight of her decision pressing down on her. The very air in the room seemed to crackle with tension, the walls closing in around her. There was no escape from the truth anymore. Not from the curse, not from the choices she had made, and not from the undeniable pull she felt toward both Dorian and the dark forces that surrounded them.

"You're lying," she whispered, her voice trembling with the intensity of her emotions. "This is all a game to you, Isaac. You've manipulated me. All of us."

Isaac's smile twisted into something colder, something that made Lila's skin crawl. "Manipulate? No, Lila, I've simply been showing you the truth. You just refuse to see it."

Dorian's eyes flared with something dark, his body tense with barely-contained rage. "You've been playing both sides, Isaac. You've been using her, using me, for your own gain. But you're not going to win this. Not anymore."

Lila could see the conflict in Dorian's eyes, the way he was fighting to keep control. She could feel the weight of everything they had been through—the moments of tenderness, the promises made in the quiet spaces between words—but now, in this moment, she couldn't ignore the reality. The truth was

The Ultimate Choice

far darker than she had imagined. The Order was real. Isaac's words were real. And she was tied to it all.

A cold shiver ran down her spine as Isaac took a step forward, his presence like a shadow that threatened to swallow her whole. He was so close now that she could feel his breath on her skin, his scent sharp, like iron and smoke.

"You don't have to make this choice alone, Lila," Isaac murmured, his voice a velvet thread of temptation. "You never did."

Her heart pounded in her chest, her breath coming in shallow bursts. She couldn't help it. She felt the pull of his words, the power he held over her, even as she loathed it. She wanted to believe him. She wanted to believe that there was a way out, a way to end this madness.

But then she turned her gaze back to Dorian, and something inside her hardened. The truth was clearer now than it had ever been. She had to choose. Her heart had already chosen him.

"Dorian..." she whispered, her voice barely audible, trembling. "What do we do now?"

Dorian's eyes softened, and for a moment, she saw the man she had come to trust, the man who had promised to help her navigate the darkness. His gaze was steady, unwavering, despite the storm that raged in his chest.

"We fight," he said simply. His voice was calm, but there was a fire behind it, a determination that pushed through the suffocating darkness. "We fight because there's still hope. For you. For us."

Lila's heart stuttered in her chest, and a wave of emotions flooded through her—fear, longing, hope. She wanted to believe him, but the weight of Isaac's words lingered, like a cloud that refused to dissipate. There was no turning back now. They had pushed too far into the heart of this twisted world. The curse was a part of her now, and so was Dorian, whether they liked it or not.

Isaac took another step forward, his smile cold and knowing. "You can't hide from your fate, Lila," he said, his voice carrying a strange sense of finality. "You can't fight what you are."

Dorian's jaw tightened. "If you think I'm going to let you take her from me, you're wrong," he growled, stepping forward, positioning himself between Isaac and Lila, his eyes dark with fury.

But Isaac merely chuckled, a sound so empty and cruel that Lila felt it reverberate in her bones. "You're a fool, Dorian. The Order will have her one way or another. The ritual is already in motion."

The weight of his words landed with a sickening finality. Lila's breath caught, and she could feel her mind spiraling, the walls closing in around her. The reality of what Isaac had said—it was too much. Too much to comprehend.

"Dorian…" she said, her voice barely a whisper. "What is the

The Ultimate Choice

ritual? What happens if I don't—if I don't go with him?"

Dorian's gaze softened, and for the first time, she saw the true depth of the pain in his eyes. He wanted to protect her, she knew that. But there was nothing he could do. Not anymore.

"The ritual is meant to bind you to the curse, Lila," he said quietly. "It's meant to force you to choose—choose between the Order, choose between the power that comes with it, or choose to break free. But breaking free comes at a price. It's never been about the curse alone. It's about you and your bloodline."

Lila's chest tightened. "My bloodline?" she whispered.

Dorian nodded slowly. "You are the key. The curse can only be broken by one of your blood. But there's another way. A darker way. The Order wants to use you to strengthen their power, to bind the curse to the world forever. They need you to choose—their version of power or the freedom to end it all."

Isaac's voice cut through the tension like a blade. "It's true, Lila. You belong to the Order. You always have. Your blood is the final piece to completing the ritual. And the power you'll wield…" He trailed off, his eyes gleaming with hunger. "It will be everything."

Lila's stomach churned, the weight of his words sinking deep into her bones. She felt the pressure of their expectations, the weight of the curse, the promises made to her. She felt it all, like a tether pulling her in a thousand different directions. She wanted to run. To scream. To hide. But there was no place left to hide.

"Dorian," she whispered, her voice breaking as she looked into his eyes, searching for some shred of hope, something to hold onto. "I don't know what to do."

Dorian stepped closer, his hand reaching out to cup her face. His touch was gentle, but there was a strength in it that steadied her, that grounded her in this moment. He leaned in, his forehead resting against hers.

"You don't have to do it alone," he whispered. "We'll face it together."

The words felt like a promise, a vow that she could hold onto. The storm of emotions inside her subsided just a little. The path ahead was still unclear, still dangerous, but with Dorian by her side, it felt like maybe—just maybe—she wasn't completely lost.

Isaac's voice sliced through the air again, more insistent this time. "Choose, Lila. Choose now."

Lila took a deep breath, her heart thundering in her chest. The room felt impossibly small, the weight of the decision pressing down on her shoulders. There was no turning back, not from the curse, not from the bloodline, not from the choices that had already been made for her.

And yet, in that moment, a flicker of clarity sparked in her chest. She wasn't just a pawn in someone else's game. She wasn't just the key to the curse.

She was Lila. And she was going to choose her fate.

With a deep breath, she stepped forward, her voice trembling but strong as she spoke.

"I choose freedom," she said, her eyes locked onto Isaac's, her voice unwavering. "I choose to break the curse. And I will do it, no matter the cost."

Isaac's eyes widened, his lips curling into a snarl. "You don't know what you're saying," he spat, his voice thick with venom.

But Lila didn't back down. She was ready. Ready to face whatever came next.

The ritual was coming. And she would be the one to end it.

Eleven

The Dawn of Freedom

The storm had passed, but its aftershocks lingered, a tangible weight in the air. The world outside the inn was suffused with a strange stillness as if nature itself had drawn a deep, reluctant breath and held it in its chest. The morning sun tried to break through the clouds, but its pale light felt weak, as if afraid to fully emerge. It cast long shadows across the town of Harrow's Edge, the soft light struggling to push away the remnants of the night's turmoil.

Inside the room, the air felt heavy with expectation, and the silence was deafening. Lila stood by the window, her hands gripping the sill, her breath shallow and quick as she gazed out into the world beyond. Her heart was still racing, the adrenaline of her decision not yet spent, the weight of her choice settling deep in her bones.

The Dawn of Freedom

She had chosen freedom. She had chosen to break the curse. And yet, in the wake of her choice, she felt more uncertain than ever.

Behind her, Dorian moved silently, his presence a constant in the space between them. She could feel the pull of him, the warmth of his body, the quiet strength he offered without a word. But she couldn't shake the nagging doubt that clung to her, the worry that the consequences of her decision were more than she could comprehend.

Dorian's voice broke through the stillness, rough with the tension of unsaid words. "We can't undo what's been done," he said softly, his tone more contemplative than before. "But we can fight."

Lila closed her eyes for a moment, taking in the truth of those words. Fight. It had always come down to that, hadn't it? No matter what they had chosen, no matter where they had ended up, it would always come down to a fight.

"You've fought before, haven't you?" she asked, her voice barely above a whisper. She turned slowly to face him, her eyes searching his. "You've always known this was coming, haven't you?"

Dorian didn't answer immediately, but his gaze held her, steady and full of something deep—something Lila couldn't quite place. He stepped closer, the space between them charged with something unspoken. The shadows of the room fell around them, the faint light from the window casting a silver glow over his face.

"It wasn't supposed to be like this," he said quietly, his voice laced with regret. "I never wanted you to get pulled into this. I never wanted you to become a part of the curse, to become part of me."

Lila felt a pang in her chest at the admission. "But I am a part of it now," she said, her voice steady despite the emotion that threatened to overtake her. "And I'm not backing down. Not from you. Not from this."

Dorian's hand reached for hers, his fingers brushing over her skin in a tender, almost reverent touch. The warmth of his skin, the quiet pressure of his hand against hers, made her pulse quicken. She could feel the heat of him, the raw energy of him, the man she had come to trust more than anyone.

"You don't know what we're up against," he said, his voice thick with something unspoken. "What you're about to face. The Order won't stop. They'll do whatever it takes to break you, to break us."

Lila's heart clenched, but she didn't pull away. Instead, she stood her ground, meeting his gaze with a determination she hadn't felt before. "I know what I'm facing, Dorian. I've faced worse than this. And I'm not letting them win."

For a long moment, there was only the sound of their breathing, the quiet rustling of the wind outside. The world felt frozen, caught in a suspended moment of uncertainty. But then, slowly,

Dorian stepped closer, his eyes softening as he closed the distance between them. His hand brushed her cheek, his touch gentle, almost tender.

Lila's breath hitched, her pulse thundering in her ears as the space between them closed. For a moment, she forgot everything—the curse, the Order, the weight of her decision. All that mattered was the feel of his hand against her skin, the heat of his body, the pull of his presence that anchored her in this moment.

"I don't want to lose you," Dorian murmured, his voice low, raw with emotion.

Lila closed her eyes, leaning into his touch, her breath slow and steady as she tried to find her bearings. She wanted to tell him that they wouldn't lose each other. That they could face this together, no matter what the cost. But the words wouldn't come. Instead, she pressed her forehead to his, their bodies barely touching but the connection between them so palpable it was as if the air itself had thickened.

"We won't lose," she whispered, her voice soft but firm. "Not if we fight."

Dorian's eyes searched hers, and in that moment, Lila saw something shift—something that made her heart ache with the weight of all they had been through. It was a silent promise, a vow made without words. No matter what came next, they would face it together.

Before she could say anything more, a soft knock at the door shattered the fragile moment between them. Lila's heart skipped a beat, and Dorian's hand dropped from her cheek as he turned toward the door, his expression instantly hardening.

"Stay behind me," he said, his voice tight with warning.

Lila nodded, her breath catching in her throat. She didn't want to face what was coming, didn't want to face what she knew was inevitable. But the knock came again, louder this time, followed by a voice—a voice that sent a cold shiver through her.

"Dorian," Isaac's voice called, smooth and taunting. "It's time."

Dorian's jaw clenched, his eyes narrowing as he turned back to Lila. "Don't open the door," he said, his voice low and filled with a quiet fury.

Lila's heart raced as she felt the weight of Isaac's words settle over her like a cloak, heavy and suffocating. She knew it wasn't over, knew that whatever they had decided, whatever they had hoped for, wasn't going to come easily. The fight had only just begun.

"I won't," she whispered, her voice a low murmur as she stepped back, her heart pounding in her chest.

Dorian's eyes lingered on her for a long moment, his gaze softening again. There was something between them—a tension, a promise—that neither of them could deny. No matter what came through that door, they would face it together.

But when the door creaked open, it wasn't Isaac who stood there. Instead, it was someone else—someone far more dangerous. The figure in the doorway was tall, cloaked in black, their face hidden in the shadows. Lila's breath caught in her throat as the figure stepped forward, their eyes gleaming with an icy light.

"You've made your choice," the figure said, their voice cold and smooth, like ice scraping across stone. "And now, you'll face the consequences."

Lila's heart stopped. She felt Dorian's hand on her arm, the pressure of it grounding her, but her mind was already racing, already thinking of the choices she had made. The ritual was no longer a distant threat. It was here, in this room, in front of them.

"Are you ready?" the figure asked, their voice cutting through the silence like a blade.

Lila's chest tightened, and for the first time, she felt the weight of what she had chosen. The fight, the curse, the power—it was all coming to a head. There was no turning back.

And as Dorian's hand gripped hers, their eyes meeting in the quiet space between them, Lila knew one thing: the fight was far from over.

But she was ready.

Twelve

Beyond the Nightfall

The wind had picked up again, sharp and biting, as if the very air were at odds with the fragile peace that had settled over Harrow's Edge. The streets below were quiet, the town still haunted by the shadows of the storm that had passed through the night before. There was something eerie about the silence now—something wrong in how the world seemed to hold its breath, waiting for something that could never be undone.

Lila stood at the window of the small, dimly lit room, her fingers lightly pressed against the cool glass. The town below was hazy in the early morning light, the shapes of the buildings distorted by the mist that clung to the streets. There was no sign of Isaac, no sign of the Order. But Lila knew better. She could feel their presence hanging like a dark cloud over the town. The calm was only temporary. And even now, standing in the quiet, she knew it would be broken.

Dorian was behind her, his presence a constant, and yet, there was an undeniable distance between them, one that neither of them could bridge. His shadow stretched out over the room, long and silent, as he stepped closer. She could feel the weight of his gaze on her and sense the questions he was too afraid to ask or answer. The tension in the room was thick enough to suffocate, but neither of them moved to change it. Not yet.

"You're still thinking about it, aren't you?" Dorian's voice broke the silence, his words low, soft, but thick with the burden of everything that had come before.

Lila didn't answer immediately, unsure of how to voice the storm of emotions inside her. She wasn't sure what she felt anymore, what she was supposed to feel. All she knew was that everything had changed the moment she had stepped into this cursed town and the ritual had begun. And now, standing on the edge of it, she felt a strange kind of numbness, a stillness that wrapped around her like a cloak.

"You don't have to do this, Lila," Dorian said again, his voice more urgent this time. He moved closer, his hand reaching for hers, but she didn't turn toward him. She couldn't. Not yet. The weight of everything—the curse, the Order, the decisions—was too much. And still, she could feel the pull between them, the bond neither could ignore.

"I'm not doing this alone, am I?" Lila whispered, her voice thick with uncertainty. She didn't look at him as she spoke; her eyes remained fixed on the distant horizon, as if searching for an answer in the mist.

"No," Dorian replied softly. His hand brushed against hers, the touch light but enough to send a tremor through her chest. "I'm with you. Every step of the way. I'll protect you."

The promise in his words was a fragile thing, something she wanted to believe, something she had to believe. But the more she thought about it, the more she realized that no matter how much Dorian wanted to shield her, the danger had already found them. It was in the air. It was in the very ground beneath their feet. The Order was coming. The curse was coming. And there was no escape.

"I don't know if I can do this," she murmured, her voice barely a whisper, lost in the wind that whispered against the windowpane. "I don't know if I can face what they want from me."

Dorian's fingers curled around hers, warm and steady. "You don't have to face it alone," he repeated, his voice a soft reassurance. He was standing close now, so close that she could feel the heat of his body against hers, could hear the steady beat of his heart. It was the sound of life, the sound of a promise. But it was a promise that was fading, slowly, as the shadows of their enemies drew nearer.

Lila closed her eyes, trying to steady her breath, trying to push away the fear that threatened to consume her. But no matter how hard she tried, the uncertainty lingered. Her bloodline, the ritual—it all circled back to her, as though she were the epicenter of this war. She had always believed she could choose her own path. But now, it felt as though the choices had already been made for her. The only thing left was whether she would embrace the power that called to her, or whether she would refuse it and risk losing everything.

"The ritual..." Lila began, her voice a little shakier than she intended. "What if I can't stop it? What if I can't break the curse?"

Dorian's fingers tightened around hers, his grip unyielding, but his expression was calm. "You're stronger than you know, Lila. The curse may be tied to your bloodline, but your heart—your choices—are yours. You can't change the past, but you can change what comes next."

Her heart stuttered in her chest as his words sank in. You can change what comes next. But could she? Could they?

A soft knock at the door interrupted her thoughts. Lila's breath caught in her throat, her pulse quickening as the reality of their situation flooded back. The knock was soft, but urgent, as though someone—no, something—was waiting for an answer.

Dorian stepped away from her, his face hardening. "Stay back," he murmured, his voice low but steady. He didn't need to say more. Lila could feel the tension in his every muscle, the way he was preparing himself for something he knew was coming. She watched as he moved toward the door, his every step a silent preparation.

Her heart thundered in her chest, and her breath caught in her throat as Dorian reached for the door, his hand lingering on the handle for a moment, as though he were weighing the consequences of whatever lay on the other side.

Then, with a quiet click, the door opened.

The figure that stood in the doorway was silhouetted by the dim light of the hall behind them. Tall and cloaked in shadows, their face hidden in the depths of their hood, they moved with a quiet grace that seemed to shimmer with menace. Lila's heart skipped a beat as she recognized them—their stance, their presence—it was unmistakable.

Isaac.

"Did you really think you could hide from us forever?" Isaac's voice was smooth and cold, a perfect reflection of the shadows that seemed to follow him. He stepped forward, his boots barely making a sound on the floor, his eyes cold and calculating as they locked onto Lila. "The ritual has already begun, Lila. There's no running from it now. No escaping what's coming."

Lila's breath caught in her throat, and she instinctively took a step back, her body reacting before her mind could process the danger. Isaac's words felt like a dark promise, a truth she had known but could never truly accept.

Dorian stepped in front of her, his body blocking hers as he faced Isaac, his expression hard with fury. "You won't get her," he growled, his voice low and dangerous.

Isaac's lips curved into a cruel smile, his eyes narrowing as he looked past Dorian to Lila. "You're too late," he said softly, his voice almost pitying. "You've always been too late, Dorian. And now, it's time for her to take her place."

Lila's chest tightened, her hands trembling as she reached for Dorian's arm. She felt the pull of the curse in her blood, felt the weight of everything that had been set in motion. And despite the fear that gripped her heart, despite the storm of emotions crashing inside her, she knew one thing.

She had to face it.

"I'm not going with you," Lila said, her voice steady despite the tremor in her hands. "I'm not going to be a pawn in your game."

Isaac's smile faltered, just for a moment, before it returned with a fierceness that sent a shiver down her spine. "You don't have a choice, Lila," he said, his voice a low murmur. "The ritual will be completed. And you will be the one to finish it."

Lila's breath caught in her throat, and as she looked at Dorian, she saw the same realization in his eyes—the same understanding of what was to come. The final battle was here. And it would be them, together, against everything.

"Then we fight," Dorian said, his voice filled with determination. He reached for Lila's hand, his grip strong and unyielding, as though he was ready to face whatever came next with her by his side.

And in that moment, standing together in the face of everything they had feared, Lila knew that they had already won.

No matter the cost.

www.ingramcontent.com/pod-product-compliance
Lightning Source LLC
LaVergne TN
LVHW020430080526
838202LV00055B/5115